For the wonderful people of Iran

The Publishers wish to acknowledge Ifeoma Onyefulu as the originator
of the series of which this book forms a part.
Ifeoma Onyefulu is the author and photographer of *A is for Africa*.

First published in Great Britain and the USA in 2011 by
Frances Lincoln Children's Books, 4 Torriano Mews,
Torriano Avenue, London NW5 2RZ
www.franceslincoln.com

A catalogue record for this book is available from the British Library.

ISBN: 978-1-84780-211-8

Set in Angie

Printed in Heshan, Guangdong, China by Leo Paper Products Ltd. in August 2011

1 3 5 7 9 8 6 4 2

I is for Iran

Shirin Adl
Kamyar Adl

FRANCES LINCOLN
CHILDREN'S BOOKS

Author's Note

Salam! My name is Shirin and I'm from Iran. My cat-shaped country sits in the Middle East bordered on one side by Armenia, Azerbaijan and Turkey, and on the other by Turkmenistan, Afghanistan and Pakistan, with the Caspian Sea to the north and the Arabian Sea and the Persian Gulf to the south. Tehran is our capital city.

Most people think Iran is a desert. There are deserts, of course, vast ones. But there are also forests and mountains, valleys and lakes, and big cities where high-rise buildings and spaghetti junctions sit alongside ancient mosques and sprawling bazaars. In Tehran, temperatures can reach as high as 43°C in summertime and as low as -15°C in winter. Our schools shut for three months in summer because nobody can study in that heat!

At school, children learn Persian (also known as Farsi). Our written alphabet is Arabic with a few extra letters added, and we write from right to left.

Nearly all Iranians are Muslim. Most are Shia Muslims, but there are also some Sunni Muslims. The rest of us are Zoroastrian, Christian, Jewish, Bahai, Mandean or Yarsani.

For hundreds of years Iran was ruled by kings, but after the 1979 revolution it became the Islamic Republic of Iran. Now, Iranian women must wear a modest covering called the *hijab* when they are out in public. This can vary from a long-sleeved shirt and a tiny headscarf to a black *chador* covering them from head to toe.

My husband Kamyar and I now live in England, but we go back home whenever we can to eat Chelo-kabab, ski in the mountains and visit our friends and family.

is for Ajil – nuts, seeds and dried fruits. Children munch them on their way to school and we offer them heaped on plates to guests. We buy special mixes for weddings, Bonfire Night and the longest night of the year.

is for Bazaar or market, often a maze of indoor corridors and narrow alleyways. Each bazaar is split into different areas selling similar types of goods. Tehran's Grand Bazaar is said to be the biggest bazaar in the world!

is for Chelo-kabab, our national dish. *Chelo* is rice — soaked, boiled, drained and steamed with oil or butter. The *kabab* is made from tender, juicy pieces of lamb or minced meat cooked over a hot barbeque. We serve it with grilled tomatoes, raw onions, fresh herbs and *doogh*, a salty drink of yogurt and water.

is for Daf — a drum shaped like a big tambourine, covered on one side with stretched goatskin. Small ring-chains are fitted all the way round at the back of the drum. They create a wonderful *swooshing* sound that makes a perfect background for the soothing rhythms of the daf.

is for Eid Norouz, our New Year and the official start of spring. On 21st March we decorate a table with seven things beginning with *Sin* (the letter 'S' in Persian), adding a book to symbolise knowledge and painted boiled eggs to represent new life. After thirteen days celebrating with our family and friends, we go out into the park or countryside to avoid any bad luck that goes with the first 13 of the year!

is for Faloodeh – a traditional dessert made of corn or rice noodles in rose water and sugar. We eat it frozen with lemon juice or fruity syrup. Faloodeh is one of the oldest frozen desserts in the world, but it's still as popular as ever.

is for Ghahveh khaneh or coffee house, a traditional Iranian cafe. We go there to relax and drink tea, meet friends and smoke water-pipes. The walls are often decorated with scenes from folk tales or religious stories.

 is for Handicrafts. Some of the techniques used here have hardly changed over thousands of years, passed down from parent to child and from master to apprentice. Our many beautiful crafts include textiles, metalwork, woodwork, jewellery, leather, glass, miniature paintings and pottery.

is for Iran, the country I love for its delicious food, poetry and art, but most of all for its big-hearted people. Iran has a population of over 76 million people and is divided into 31 provinces, each with its own capital city and governor. Tehran, the country's capital, is also the largest city. Our biggest exports are oil and gas, carpets and pistachio nuts.

is for Javaher – jewellery. They say that diamonds are a girl's best friend – but in the Islamic world gold is a girl's best friend and men are forbidden to wear it! Instead, Iranian men wear one or two chunky silver rings like those displayed here by a ring-seller.

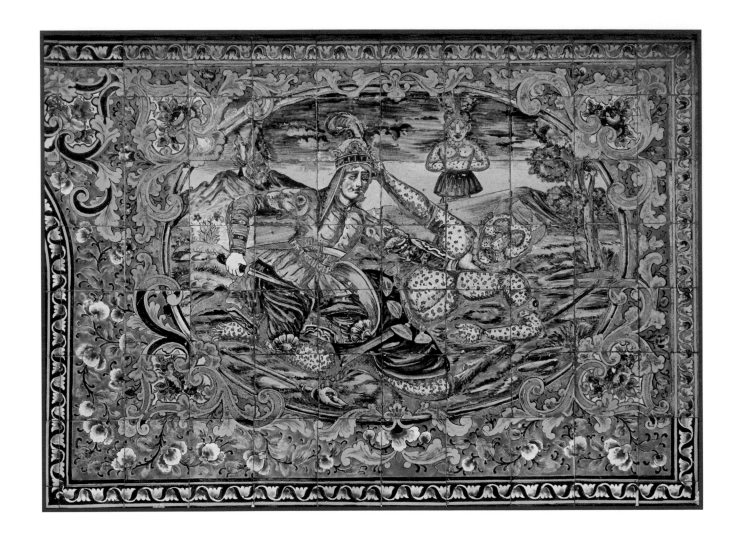

is for Kaashi or tile. We use tiles to decorate many of our buildings. This tiled scene from the Golestan Palace in Tehran shows Iran's national hero Rostam fighting the White Demon – an adventure which every Iranian reads about in our country's epic poem *The Shahnameh*.

is for the Love and affection
we feel for each other.
Iranians are warm people,
passionate by nature and
fond of big displays of
affection. Our hellos and
goodbyes are followed by
lots of kisses and hugs –
even when we have only
been apart for a few hours!

 is for Masjed or mosque, where people go for daily prayers and gather on religious occasions. There are many old and beautiful mosques in Iran, including the Vakil Mosque in Shiraz (top) and the Imam Khomeini Mosque in Isfahan (bottom).

is for Naan or bread. Traditional bakeries usually bake three times a day – in the early morning, just before noon and in the evening. People queue outside to buy bread hot from the oven for their meals. What's left is hung up on nails to cool down and then sold to customers later.

is for Olagh or donkey.
Modern cars and trucks are
fine for transporting goods,
but when it comes to steep,
narrow, rocky mountain
roads, the olagh is still
the number one carrier.
They are often decorated
with colourful beads.

 is for Plane trees which grow on either side of many of our streets. They love our hot summers and cold winters, and we love the shade they provide for us.

is for Quiet in the afternoon when people are taking their naps. A cool, shady courtyard like this is a wonderful place to rest on a hot summer day. Most shops and businesses are closed between one and three o'clock, but they reopen later on and many stay open until late at night.

is for Rugs. Persian rugs are famous worldwide for their craftsmanship, stunning patterns and vibrant colours. Handmade rugs are sometimes sold for vast amounts of money and their value increases the older they become. The man in this picture is rubbing the rug to make sure it is smooth.

is for Siose-pol, "the Bridge of Thirty-Three" – a beautiful old bridge in Isfahan. It is 298 metres long with a row of 33 arches along each side. Siose-pol crosses the River Zayandeh which starts in the Zagros mountains in west Iran and ends in Lake Gavkhooni, south-east of Isfahan.

is for Takht-e Jamshid – better known to the world as Persepolis. Built over 2,500 years ago, this awe-inspiring place was once the ceremonial capital of the Persian Empire. Takht-e Jamshid stands just outside the modern city of Shiraz.

is for Uncles (not forgetting aunts and cousins too). In Iran
our extended family is important to us and we try to see
our relations as often as we can.

is for Vitamins in the vegetable and fruit juices and smoothies we like to buy from stalls by the side of the road. My favourite is carrot juice and Kamyar's is pomegranate juice.

is for Water – essential in a hot, dry country like Iran. In summer, shiny dispensers of ice and water are put out in the streets by kind citizens so that thirsty passers-by can help themselves to a drink.

is the miX of races in our country: Persians in central Iran, Azeris in the north-west, Kurds in the west, Talesh, Gilaki and Mazandarani people in the north, Turkmens in the north-east, Lors and Qashqais in the south-west, Iranian Arabs in the south and Balooch people in the south-east. There are also many Jewish Iranians, Afghans and Armenians living here.

is for Ya Hagh. It means "the truth". The dervishes – holy men like this, known for their poverty and simple lives who are forever seeking truth – always call out "Ya Hagh!" when they take their leave.

is for Zourkhaneh or traditional gymnasium where men exercise to the rhythm of drum and bells. These men are highly respected for their bravery, religious devotion and helping other people.

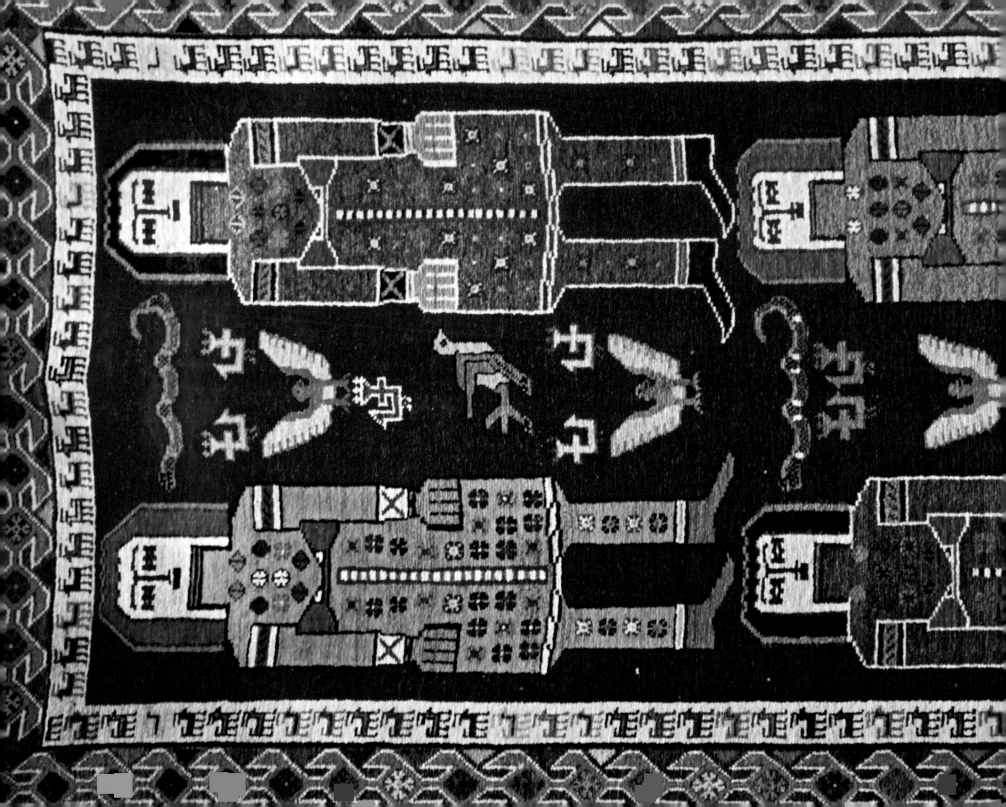